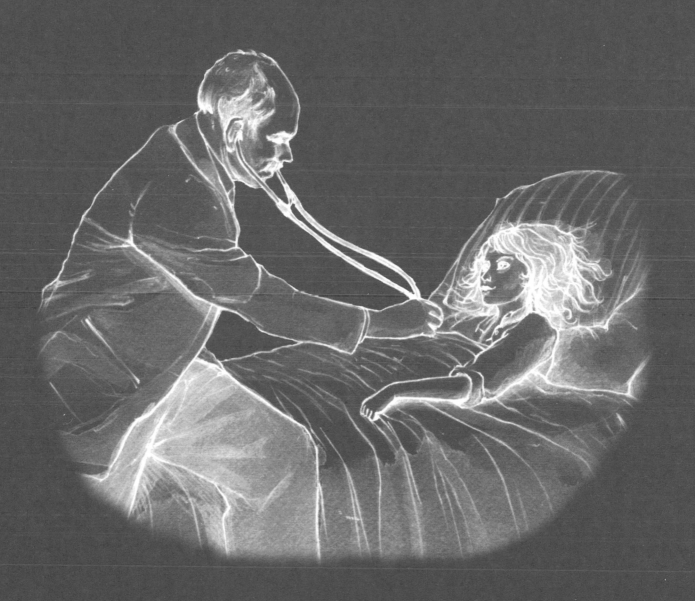

W9-BMX-152

Righting Wrongs

The Story of Norman Bethune

by

John Wilson

Napoleon Publishing
Toronto Ontario Canada

Napoleon Publishing gratefully acknowledges
the support of the Canada Council
for our publishing program.

Printed in Hong Kong

For Fiona

National Library of Canada Cataloguing in Publication Data

WIlson, John (John Alexander), date—
        Righting wrongs: the story of Norman Bethune

(Stories of Canada)
ISBN 0-929141-71-7

        1. Bethune, Norman 1890-1939—Juvenile literature. 2. Surgeons—Canada—Biography—
Juvenile literature. I. Title II. Series: Stories of Canada (Toronto, Ont.)

R464.B4W543 2001   617'092   C2001-901971-8

Righting Wrongs

The Story of Norman Bethune

by

John Wilson

Illustrations by Liz Milkau

Napoleon Publishing

A Race of Men

On March 1, 1546, Cardinal David Beaton (as Bethune was spelled in Scotland in those days) watched from a window of St. Andrews castle in Scotland as George Wishart was burned at the stake for criticizing the Roman Catholic church. David Beaton was the most powerful man in Scotland. By burning Wishart, he was trying to halt the new ideas that were sweeping his country and his church. He failed. On May 29 a band of Protestants broke into the castle, killed Beaton and threw his body from the very window he had sat at on that fiery afternoon less than three months before.

David Beaton died trying to prevent change. Almost 400 years later, his ancestor, Norman Bethune, was to die trying to bring about change.

Dr. Norman Bethune talked proudly of his ancestry. He claimed they included: a Norman nobleman who served William the Conqueror; a poet who wrote verse over 800 years ago; a Sixteenth Century Scottish Cardinal who enjoyed watching as Protestants were burned alive beneath his castle window; a handmaid to Mary, Queen of Scots; a surgeon who fought at the Battle of Culloden Moor in Scotland in 1746; and a Presbyterian minister who was imprisoned during the American Revolution.

They all lived in times very different from our own, and each had an effect on the times in which he or she lived. However, none worked as hard, or in so many different ways, to change and improve the lot of their fellows as did the Bethune who was born in a small Ontario town in 1890.

Getting Sick, Getting Well

Bethune operating in Montreal

Universal medicare like Bethune dreamed of came late to Canada. Saskatchewan was the first province to introduce it in 1962. All Canadians were covered by 1971, almost forty years after Bethune fought for it.

Today, if you get sick, you go to a doctor, and he or she works to make you well again. In Norman Bethune's day, if you got sick and had enough money, you went to a doctor, and he or she worked to make you well. If you got sick and were poor, you either stayed sick or found one of the few doctors like Bethune who would treat you for free.

Norman Bethune had a dream of medical care for everyone, regardless of how much money they had. He worked in clinics which treated unemployed and poor people for free. He wrote articles and letters to politicians saying how he thought medical care in Canada should be organized. He gave speeches to other doctors telling them what he saw as wrong in the way they treated the sick.

We take medical care for granted today, but if it were not for Norman Bethune and others like him, we might still have to stay sick if we couldn't afford to pay a doctor.

Egyptian kings more than 2000 years ago suffered from tuberculosis. Tuberculosis is caused by bacteria, which an English doctor, Benjamin Marten, in 1720 called "wonderfully minute living creatures". They are passed from person to person in saliva—if someone with tuberculosis coughs in your face, you can catch the disease.

Tuberculosis usually affects the lungs and, in the days before antibiotics, it was often fatal. During the First World War, more Canadians died at home of tuberculosis than were killed in the battles in Europe. The disease used to spread rapidly in the dirty, overcrowded buildings where poor families were forced to live.

Since the poor could not afford to go and see a doctor or take time off work for treatment, they stayed at home, gradually infecting the rest of their family. Bethune argued that if the living conditions of the poor were improved, the spread of tuberculosis could be stopped.

The White Plague

In Bethune's day, antibiotics had not been discovered. There is a disease called tuberculosis. It was also once known as the White Plague, and it killed thousands of Canadians every year. Bethune himself had tuberculosis in 1926. He was lucky; he recovered. But because of his experience with the disease, he decided to become a chest surgeon and help others with the disease.

For ten years he worked tirelessly operating on and saving patients who were so sick that other doctors had given up hope. He also improved and invented surgical instruments to make his work easier. Some of them are still in use in hospitals today.

Bethune saw a disease that had no cure. He did not discover a cure, but he worked hard to change the way patients were treated. As a result, many hundreds of people who might otherwise have died lived long and happy lives.

3

A Better World

In the 1930s, Hitler was in power in Germany and Mussolini in Italy. These men led Fascist governments. Many people in Canada admired the Fascists because they thought that they would bring order to the country. Bethune disagreed. He saw that Fascism did not help the poor and that anyone who spoke out against the Fascists in Europe was thrown in prison. Bethune saw that if the world was going to change for the better, Fascism would have to be stopped. He used his talents as a doctor and a surgeon in Canada, Spain and China to help anyone who was fighting against Fascism.

When he was working in Detroit in 1925, Bethune was called out one night to attend to a poor woman who was giving birth. He was taken to a disused railway carriage, in which a large family lived in poverty. He delivered the baby and turned down the husband's offer of a dollar payment. It was the man's entire savings.

Bethune did not think that the baby would live very long in the conditions in the carriage. It made him very angry. He realized that a job for the baby's father, paying as little as $20 a week, would do more for the health of the family than all his medical skill and training.

From that time on, Bethune fought against injustice and worked to change a system which he saw as the cause of the poor family's troubles.

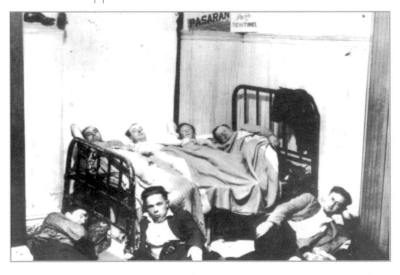

Poor workers often had to share one room between them.

Birth

The town of Gravenhurst existed because of the logging in the forests around it. It was surrounded by 17 mills and was often called the "Sawdust City." By 1890 it was known across Canada for the boats that were built there. By coincidence, considering Bethune's later work with tuberculosis, Gravenhurst was also home to the Muskoka Cottage Sanatorium for patients who were recovering from the disease.

Henry Norman Bethune was born on an overcast Monday in March, 1890. Henry, as he was known when he was little, was the middle of three children. His sister, Janet Louise, was already two years old in 1890 and his brother, Malcolm Goodwin, would not be born until 1892. The family lived in a ten-room house in Gravenhurst, Ontario, about 160 kilometres north of Toronto. The house is now a museum, but at that time it was reserved for the town's Presbyterian Minister, Henry Norman's father. The Norman in Bethune's name came from his grandfather who was living with the family in Gravenhurst. Although his grandfather died when Henry Norman was only two years old, the old man had a very strong influence on the boy.

The Bethune house in Gravenhurst, Ontario, is now a museum that is open to the public.

Grandfather Norman

Norman Bethune's grandfather was Dean of Trinity Medical School in Toronto in 1856, when the school decided to prevent students who were not members of the Anglican Church from attending. This unfairness so enraged Grandfather Norman that he resigned. So many doctors followed his example that the school had to close down. It did not reopen for fifteen years, and when it did, there was no restriction on who could attend. Grandfather Norman was rehired as Dean.

Henry Norman turned out to be much like his grandfather—both were doctors, both were artists and writers, and both were very strongwilled. Grandfather Norman was sixty-eight when Bethune was born and died only two years later. Yet Bethune remembered the old man vividly and often mimicked his limping walk.

Probably much of what Bethune learned of his grandfather came from family stories. In the days before radio, television and video games, families often sat and talked in the evenings, telling stories of their ancestors. Grandfather Norman had an exciting life, travelling all over the world and getting into trouble for his outspoken views. He was probably the subject of many tales in front of the fire, and his grandson took many of them to heart. When young Henry Norman was eight, he announced that he wanted to be a surgeon like his grandfather. He also declared that he was to be known as Norman from then on, and he hung the old man's brass doctor's plate outside his bedroom door.

Before television

Without television, video games, the Internet, movies or even radio, families in the 1890s had to make their own entertainments. Music could be played on a wind-up gramophone or around the family piano. Card games were popular, as were games such as charades which involved the whole family. Reading, both out loud and silently, was common. In a religious house like the one Bethune grew up in, many readings would probably have been from the Bible.

Norman (on the left) with his brother and sister, 1900

Evenings in the Bethune household were spent reading, telling stories and playing games. A favourite of Norman's was a game where each of the children had to correctly pronounce and define a new word. The incentive was that if you got your word right, you got five cents. Norman became good at it and earned a lot of money this way.

Norman's other passion was rearranging the furniture in a room until he thought it looked better than before. This early sign of his artistic talent must have been annoying for his parents, but they tolerated it well.

Life with father

At the age of twenty-one, Malcolm Bethune turned his back on his family and set off around the world to seek his fortune. For years he travelled and tried different business ventures. They all failed. Eventually, he ended up in Hawaii growing oranges. There he met a missionary, Elizabeth Ann Goodwin. Malcolm fell in love and decided that he too wanted to become a preacher. He returned to Canada, became a Presbyterian minister and married Elizabeth. His first posting as a minister was to Gravenhurst.

Norman and his father Malcolm fought a lot. Malcolm was stern and attempted to impose discipline on his son. On one occasion, he pushed Norman's face into the ground and forced him to eat dirt to teach him humility.

Norman rebelled at his father's strictness. As a result, they used to have a lot of arguments. These arguments were loud and angry. Malcolm always apologized afterwards. Later in life, Norman said that he and his father used to have their "usual hate together."

Malcolm's strictness left Norman with a lifelong urge to push limits—to ignore what other people told him were the rules. This made him very adventurous, but it must have been difficult for his friends, who never quite knew what Norman was going to do next.

Malcolm Bethune with his children, horse and buggy in pre-car days

Life with mother

Elizabeth was born in London, England. Her father was a cabinet maker. By the age of ten she had a very strong belief in God and spent her free time handing out religious leaflets in the streets. Like Malcolm, she also left home at twenty-one, but not to search for fame and fortune. Elizabeth went to Hawaii to become a missionary and to teach the people there about her God. Little did she know that her most important convert would be a young fortune-hunter from Canada, Malcolm Bethune.

Elizabeth wanted Norman to grow up to be just as God-fearing as Malcolm. However, she was not as strict as her husband, and Norman had fewer fights with her. When he was at school learning about Charles Darwin's Theory of Evolution, Elizabeth used to put religious pamphlets between the pages of Darwin's famous book, *The Origin of Species*. Norman responded by placing a copy of the book under his mother's pillow while she slept. In the morning, she threw the book in the wood stove.

From his mother, Norman received a sense of justice and a desire to help people less fortunate than himself. This produced a gentle side to his character which helped balance his desire to break the rules.

The Bethune children with Elizabeth, 1904. Norman is second from the right.

Wilderness Boy

If you wanted to go anywhere in rural Ontario in the 1890s, you walked, went by canoe or used a horse either to ride or pull a carriage. There were no paved roads or motor cars. It took a lot longer to get from one place to another, but the pace of life was much slower.

Because his father moved around a lot, Norman lived in many small towns in Ontario as he grew up. Before he was seventeen, he had lived in Gravenhurst, Beaverton, Toronto, Aylmer, Blind River, Sault Ste. Marie and Owen Sound. Summers were often spent back at Gravenhurst. Most of the towns Norman lived in were small logging communities surrounded by wilderness. This gave him a chance to explore to his heart's content. It also made him fit and self-sufficient. Norman loved swimming, fishing and running on floating logs like the local lumberjacks.

In his love of the woods and wild places, Norman was like his great-grandfather Angus, who worked as a fur trader in both the Northwest Company and the Hudson's Bay Company.

A Brave Boy

Summer holidays in the small towns Norman grew up in were spent outdoors as much as possible. The woods and lakes were a playground where a boy could learn about nature by experiencing it up close.

Growing up surrounded by wilderness presented Norman with many opportunities for adventure. One winter, he and some friends were playing on the ice when it gave way and a boy fell through. While the others fled to the safety of the shore, Norman edged out to the hole and rescued the boy.

On other occasions, Norman's adventurous spirit got him into trouble. One summer, at Honey Harbour on Georgian Bay, he watched as his father swam across the bay. The next day, without telling anybody, Norman attempted the same feat and was only saved from drowning by his father's appearance in a boat. It was a foolhardy thing to do, but Norman was stubborn. The next year the family returned to the same spot and Norman repeated his escapade—but this time he made it all the way.

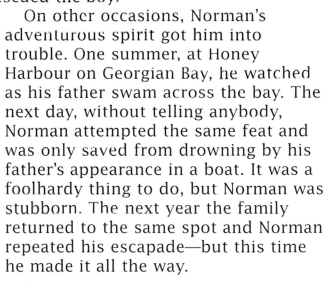

Norman enjoyed outdoor activity. Here he poses (centre) with teammates from the Owen Sound Collegiate Institute soccer team, around 1905 when he would have been fifteen years old.

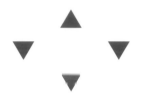

The Butterfly Collector

Hobbies were important to children in the 1890s. Collecting was common. Norman collected butterflies, but he could have collected many things: coins, stamps, seashells or lead soldiers. His sister would be more likely to have done needlepoint as a hobby.

One of Norman's hobbies was butterfly collecting. This is normally thought of as a quiet, safe thing to do, but not where Norman was concerned. On one occasion, he spotted a nice specimen at the top of a cliff. With his brother Malcolm following, Norman set off up the cliff face. Halfway, Malcolm said he was scared. Norman left him, climbed the cliff, caught the butterfly and rescued Malcolm on the way down.

It did not always end happily, however. On two similar occasions, Norman fell and broke his leg. Probably he enjoyed the challenge of catching the butterfly as much or more than having the butterfly itself.

Toronto Life

In 1900, Toronto was growing rapidly. In sixty years it had changed from a town of 9,000 people to a city of 300,000. Its many meat packing plants had earned it the nickname "Hogtown." The streets would have been busy and lively, but they would also have been smelly. There were few motor cars, and horses still did most of the work carrying people and hauling goods between the railway station and the markets. The smell of horse would have been very strong, and you would have to watch where you stepped when you were crossing the street.

In 1904, when Norman was in Sault Ste. Marie, a fire started in a Toronto necktie shop. Before it was put out, it had destroyed a hundred buildings and caused millions of dollars in damage. Many of the old buildings in downtown Toronto today date from the rebuilding after the fire.

Even during the two short spells when his father was posted to Toronto, a long way from Norman's beloved wilderness, the boy managed to find excitement. Norman was only six the first time the family moved to Toronto; nevertheless, he decided to explore the city just as he might the woods around a small town. Without telling anyone, he set off. By late afternoon the police, alerted by his now frantic mother, were combing the city for the lost boy. As it got dark, Norman calmly walked in the front door, having walked the full ten miles from one side of the city to the other.

City of Toronto Archives, SC244, Item 24

A typical Toronto street scene in the early 20th century

The Young Doctor

Today, if you want to see what a cow's bones look like, you could look up a specialist book in the library, or probably find something on the Internet. In Bethune's day in rural Ontario, if you wanted to see what a cow's bones looked like, you had to do what Norman did, find a cow's leg and boil the meat off the bone. It was a lot more work than surfing the Internet, but it would have been a better way to learn.

Norman was never in any doubt that he wanted to be a doctor like his grandfather. By way of practice, he would cut up insects, chicken bones and anything else he thought might be interesting to look at.

Once, his mother noticed a strange smell in the house. Tracing it to the attic, she discovered Norman busily cutting the meat off a cow's leg he had just finished boiling. In answer to her horrified question, Norman replied that he was only removing the flesh so that he could examine the bone more closely. From then on, there was always a collection of assorted bones laid out along the back fence to dry.

Norman's curiosity was an important part of his character. Throughout his life, he studied things to see how they worked. It didn't matter what the things were, surgical instruments or types of government, Norman Bethune wanted to know how they worked. Often, once he had examined them, he could suggest a way they could be improved.

In a rural schoolhouse at the turn of the century, every grade would be present in one room, and one teacher would teach them all. Sometimes, if the class were large, the older children would help teach the younger ones, but mostly each grade did its own work. When you finished the work of one grade, you simply moved on to the work of the next grade, even if it was in the middle of a year. Summer holidays were long so that the children would have time at home to help around the farm at the busiest time.

Educating the Boy

Because the family moved around so much, Norman went to a lot of different schools. In Toronto, they would be large and well-organized, but in many of the towns they were probably just one classroom where all the grades were taught by a single teacher.

We don't know how Norman did at school, but a lot of the time he probably wished he were outdoors or examining bones. In any case, he did all right and graduated from Owen Sound Collegiate in 1907. The first thing he did was take a job in the wilderness at a logging camp.

One-room schoolhouses like this one, where several grades learned together, were a way of life in small communities well into the twentieth century.

The Logger

Life in a logging camp was hard. Loggers did not have all the machinery that there is today, and most of the work had to be done by hand. Trees were felled by two men who stood on boards notched into the tree trunk. This was to raise them above the wide part of the trunk near the ground. Each took one end of a long saw, and, while one pushed, the other pulled. It was important that the two men worked in the same rhythm, and pairs of men who worked well together would stay together as long as possible.

Logging camps in the bush in 1907 were rough places. The work was hard, but Norman enjoyed the independence. A year in the camps around Algoma made him tough and strong. They were characteristics he was to need often in the life he was to choose.

Logging in the young Bethune's time was hard work, all done by hand. The men on the left are cutting lengths, which would then be collected and pulled in loads by horses (above).

17

School discipline in 1909 was harsh by today's standards. There were no school counsellors, and many of the students were used to living a life much harder than students today. Teachers would use any method they could to maintain order. The most common was the use of a narrow leather strap which was used across the palms of disobedient students' hands. Six or more hits with the strap would be very painful. Other teachers used a cane on the student's backside. Either way, the idea was to impose order and discipline by inflicting pain.

The Teacher

In January, 1909, when Norman was only nineteen and just recently out of school himself, he took a job teaching. The school at Edgely, just north of Toronto, had only one room and the students had discipline problems. Norman was a strict disciplinarian, and on many days there was a line of students at the end of school awaiting the strap from the new teacher.

Sometimes there were fights between the students and Norman. Once, the students even brought in an outsider to fight Norman. It was a mistake. Norman was a good boxer, and he was wiry and fit after his year logging. He easily knocked down the students' champion, and that was the end of his discipline problems.

The teaching post at Edgely lasted only six months, for which Norman was paid $269.00. He never went back to formal school teaching, but he taught whenever he could and always felt that education was a vital part of improving the world.

University and another way of teaching

Alfred Fitzpatrick believed that education should be available everywhere, "on the farm, in the bush, on the railway, and in the mine." In 1899 he founded the Reading Camp Association to try and teach people who could not get into school. The students were mostly adults and they were mostly taught English. In 1919, the name was changed to Frontier College. Frontier College still exists today, and now works with children and teens, people in prison, living on the streets or with special needs—in fact, anyone who cannot, for one reason or another, get to school.

Norman Bethune must have liked the idea that the teachers should go to the pupils rather than the other way around. All through his life, he practised the idea that doctors should go where they were needed rather than wait for the sick and wounded to come to them.

After Edgely, Bethune enrolled in the University of Toronto to study Physiology and Biochemistry. He passed his courses, but his marks were not good, and he was bored. He missed his beloved wilderness. After two years he found an answer.

In 1911, Bethune joined the Reading Camp Association. The arrangement was that Bethune and other students would work at remote logging camps during the day. In exchange for free accommodation, they would spend their evenings teaching the loggers, many of whom were recent immigrants without good English skills. It suited Bethune perfectly. He was in the wilderness, working hard and doing something worthwhile. He even had to be self-sufficient, on occasion fixing a broken phonograph or setting a man's broken leg.

Norman (centre with legs apart) with loggers during his Reading Camp Association days, 1911

19

Back to University

On June 28, 1914, Archduke Franz Ferdinand, the heir to the Austrian throne, and his wife, Sophie, were shot and killed as they were driven through the streets of Sarajevo. As a result, Austria went to war with Serbia and, because they all had signed treaties to help each other if attacked, within weeks, Russia, Germany, France, Britain and Canada were all also at war. The First World War had begun.

The First World War (or the Great War, as it was then known) left Europe's cities and villages ruined, and countless lives were lost. Bethune's was not the only young life sadly interrupted, but unlike millions of other young men, he was lucky enough to survive.

The Reading Camp Association only operated in the winter, so Bethune spent the summer of 1912 travelling and working as a reporter for the Winnipeg Telegram newspaper. In the fall, he found there were no positions with the college, so Bethune returned to the University of Toronto to study medicine. This time around he did better and his marks improved. but things were happening on the other side of the world that would disrupt his education once more.

The Stretcher Bearer

The job of a stretcher bearer was to remove wounded soldiers from the danger of the front lines to the safety of an aid station, where they could be treated and moved even farther away by train or ambulance. The work was very hard; the stretcher often had to be lifted above the bearer's heads to get around tight corners in the trench, and it was dangerous, since the bearers sometimes had to leave the safety of the trenches and expose themselves to the fire of the enemy. By the time a wounded soldier had been carried to an aid station, the stretcher bearer would be covered in sweat, his muscles would ache unbearably and his feet would be painfully blistered. Then he would have to turn around, go back into danger, and do it all over again.

Norman joined the army as a stretcher bearer on September 8, 1914. After his training with the Number Two Field Ambulance Medical Corps, he went over to Europe to join the First Canadian Division near the town of Ypres in Belgium. A few miles away, another Canadian doctor was working. His name was John McCrae, and he would soon write the most famous Canadian poem of the First World War, "In Flanders Fields". The Canadians were fighting beside the French, Belgian and British armies to stop the German army which had invaded France in 1914.

The soldiers of both sides lived underground in trenches and dugouts, sometimes only a few tens of metres from the enemy. When someone was wounded, it was the stretcher bearer's job to move the soldier back to safety, where his wounds could be treated. It was difficult and dangerous work.

In Battle

Shells and bullets were not the only danger to the Canadians at Ypres. During the battle in which Bethune was wounded, the Germans used poisoned gas for the first time. It was chlorine that drifted on the wind across the battlefield. If a soldier was caught in it, his eyes, mouth and throat would begin to burn. Then he would begin coughing. The natural instinct was to huddle down, but chlorine is heavier than air and collects in the bottoms of trenches or in any hole in the ground, exactly the places a soldier of the First World War felt safest. If the soldier couldn't get his gas mask on or run from the gas, he would suffocate.

A shelled church in Ypres, Belgium. Very little was left untouched by bombing during those terrible years.

In April 1915, the Germans attacked the Canadians in front of Ypres, in Belgium. For a week, Bethune worked furiously helping the wounded and carrying them back to safety. On April 29, he was working when a shell exploded nearby. A piece of metal went through Bethune's left leg. In agony, he now made the journey he had sent so many other wounded men on—to the aid station, hospital, train station and ship over to Britain. Within two days of being wounded, Bethune was in hospital in Cambridge, England. Six months later, he had recovered and was back in Canada.

Effects of War

In a letter home, Bethune described how he felt about the war: "The slaughter has begun to appall me. I've begun to question whether it is worth it. Attached to the medical services, I see little of war's glory, and most of war's waste."

Although his experiences in the first World War were brief, they had a lasting effect on young Norman Bethune. He never forgot the agonies of the wounded soldiers or the waste of all the young lives. Most vividly, he never forgot the many young men he saw bleed to death because, in 1915, there was no way that they could be given a transfusion of blood anywhere near the battle.

Canadian soldiers try to keep their spirits up in the trenches of France. Bethune would have worked in these dirty, dangerous conditions.

Back to School

Norman joined the Navy because a young woman gave him a white feather. During the First World War, the white feather was a symbol of cowardice. Young women presented it to men of military age if they were not in a soldier's uniform. This was to try and shame them into joining the army. It was very unfair since, often, soldiers recovering from wounds or on leave did not walk around in uniform. The white feather made Bethune feel bad, but he was not a coward.

Norman poses on board a ship in the navy at age twenty-eight. The writing says "Norman Bethune and friend, Jan. 20/18".

When he arrived back in Canada, Norman Bethune returned to the University of Toronto to complete his training as a doctor. He graduated in 1916 and, after working for a short time as a doctor in Stratford, Ontario, he joined the Royal Navy as a surgeon. He worked hard curing the sick sailors on his ship, but he didn't see any more fighting like that around Ypres.

After the War

After the First World War ended in 1918, Bethune had trouble settling down. He worked at the famous Hospital for Sick Children in London, England, as a small town doctor back in Stratford, Ontario, and at various hospitals in London and Edinburgh, Scotland. He even tried joining the air force. Nothing suited him, although he was lively and well-liked.

In Stratford, he threw parties for the children of the town. Once, he was visiting a sick farmer, and the man's wife was upset because there was no one to milk the cows. Bethune treated the sick man, then rolled up his sleeves, picked up the milking pail and strode out to attend to the cows. It was no wonder that, when it was time for Bethune to leave, the townspeople collected money to pay him to stay as their doctor. Bethune refused. There were too many other exciting places to go and things to do.

Norman Bethune was not the only person who couldn't settle down after the First World War. The surviving soldiers had been through so much, seen so many real-life horrors and lost so many friends, that many felt surprised that they were still alive. A world at peace seemed odd, and they tried to live every day as if it might be their last.

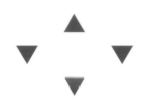

Falling in Love

There is a story of a medieval knight who fell in love with a beautiful Lady. To test his love for her, the Lady threw a rose into a lion's den and asked the knight to retrieve it. The knight did so, but then he mounted his horse and rode away. Bethune, like the lady, didn't realize that true love doesn't need to be tested.

When Bethune first met the nineteen-year-old Frances Campbell Penney in Edinburgh in 1920, he was attracted by her lilting Scottish accent. In fact, he said later that he fell in love "at first sound." Frances was shy and cautious, but she was captivated by the brash young Canadian doctor. Her mother, however, was not quite so impressed with the penniless young man.

Norman courted Frances for three years. Then she inherited some money from an uncle. At last she could afford to leave home. On August 13, 1923, they were married in London. The first Norman's family heard of it was a telegram: "Married Honeymoon Here Very Happy Writing." To Frances, Norman promised: "Now I can make your life a misery, but I'll never bore you." Then he whisked his new bride off on a whirlwind six-month tour of Europe which used up most of Frances' inheritance.

Bethune had a strange need to test his new bride. On a walk, shortly after they were married, they came to a small ravine. Bethune told Frances to jump across it, even though they could easily walk around. When Frances asked why, Bethune replied that he would rather see her dead than refuse this dangerous act. Frances did jump and Norman did later apologize, but his unreasonable request killed something in their relationship.

Settling Down
at Last?

Detroit in the 1920s was a wild town. It had trebled in size in just fourteen years and was thriving economically. But there were problems. Bethune disliked the dirt everywhere and described the city as: "Awfully squalid—terribly so. The people look...vulgar and brutal... I do wish they didn't, but they do."

In 1924, Norman opened a medical practice in Detroit. Many of his colleagues were becoming rich treating wealthy patients. Norman treated anyone who needed it, regardless of whether they could pay or not. It was a hard life, treating patients in his surgery, working at the local hospital, teaching at Detroit College of Medicine and Surgery and being called out at all hours of the night to attend to poor workers. Often his patients couldn't pay in money. The local shopkeepers paid Bethune in meat, groceries and furniture. But he still spent money wildly whenever he had it, buying good food, expensive paintings and ornaments.

By 1900, Detroit was already a bustling city. This is one of the main streets, with cable cars like those still used in Toronto.

27

A Marriage in Trouble

Bethune probably contracted tuberculosis from one of his patients. The disease was widespread amongst the poor, and they could rarely afford to pay for treatment, so they stayed at home infecting the rest of their family and, sometimes, the doctors who came to visit them. Bethune was lucky. He could afford to take time off work and have treatment, but hundreds of poor people in Detroit, and every other large city, could not. They died.

Norman and Frances in happier times.

Life in Detroit was hard for Frances. She had nothing to do while Norman was busy, and the pair was continually fighting about money. It was impossible for Bethune to save any; he wildly spent whatever money the couple had. In the fall of 1925, Frances felt she had put up with enough. She left Norman to go and stay with a friend in Nova Scotia.

Norman begged her to come back to him and, in 1926, she did. But things weren't any better. On top of the disagreements and arguments, Bethune was not well. He felt weak and became tired very easily. Frances persuaded him to go and see a doctor friend. The news was not good—Bethune had tuberculosis in one lung.

Trudeau Sanatorium

In the late nineteenth century, the only hope for a tuberculosis sufferer was rest and fresh air. To promote this, doctors began establishing sanatoria, places where patients could rest and recover. Trudeau was one of the most famous in North America. It had twenty-eight cottages, two hospitals, a library, laboratory, workshop, nurses home, chapel and post office. Two hundred staff looked after as many as 160 patients. Trudeau could not promise a cure; rather it aimed at teaching patients to live with the disease. In this it was successful. The problem for many people was that it cost $15 a week (a lot of money in 1926) for a sixth-month course. If you didn't have the money, you couldn't go.

Battles Against Tuberculosis

In December 1926, Norman Bethune entered the Trudeau Sanatorium near New York. He was upset that he and Frances were not getting along and angry that his illness was interrupting his work. On top of it all, he was ordered to rest.

Bethune was not happy when he had nothing to do, so he broke the rules. Smoking was not allowed, Bethune smoked; parties were forbidden, Bethune threw wild parties; passes out of the sanatorium were limited, so Bethune built a dummy in his bed and snuck out to the local town.

The quiet of the sanatorium was shaken by this eccentric Canadian who drank tea from a silver pot, wore a beret everywhere and walked the halls tapping his cane on the floor. But, under the bravado, Bethune was depressed. Frances said she wanted a divorce, and Norman considered suicide. But he didn't give up. His illness was something he might be able to do something about.

During the Napoleonic wars of the nineteenth century, doctors noticed that soldiers with tuberculosis who had received a non-fatal bayonet wound to the chest showed an improvement. What was happening was that the wound allowed air in between the chest wall and the lung. The lung collapsed and this helped it heal. To do this artificially was risky until x-rays allowed doctors to see what they were doing.

Sometimes air had to be pumped in to help collapse the lung. Bethune invented a machine to do this and often used it on himself in the years after he left Trudeau.

Bethune tried to be optimistic about his condition. Here he poses (far left) smiling with fellow Trudeau patients.

Not Giving Up

At Trudeau, Bethune read everything he could on tuberculosis. Eventually, he discovered a recently developed treatment called Artificial Pneumothorax. It involved collapsing the infected lung to allow it to heal. The advantage was that the patient could function normally on the other lung while the collapsed one was healing. The disadvantage was that it was a dangerous operation.

The doctors at Trudeau refused to perform it on Bethune. He persisted. At one meeting, when the doctors told him how risky the operation was, Bethune theatrically threw open his shirt and declared: "Gentlemen, I welcome the risk!"

His persistence worked. On October 27, 1927, the pneumothorax operation was performed on Bethune. On December 10, a year after he had first entered it, Bethune was released from Trudeau. He had recovered from his illness, but he had not saved his marriage. Three days before the operation to collapse his lung, Frances had obtained a divorce.

Back at work

Poor people, who could not afford to go to doctors, often allowed their tuberculosis to advance so far that sanatorium rest, even if they could afford it, would do no good. In the days before antibiotics, surgery was their only hope. Chest surgery was dangerous, and patients often died as a result. Because of this, many doctors were reluctant to perform major chest surgery, even though it might be the patient's only chance for recovery.

After his experience with tuberculosis, Bethune was determined to do what he could to help other sufferers. He went to the Royal Victoria Hospital in Montreal to study and work under Dr. Edward Archibald, a Canadian pioneer in chest surgery. Norman's life appeared to be settling down and Frances moved to Montreal to remarry him in 1929.

An artist friend painted this picture of Norman at work at Sacré-Cœur Hospital, Montreal.

"My Child"

Bethune wrote to a friend after his operation on Yvette: "My child is well. It was a very beautiful operation. I felt very happy doing it. The entire right lung was removed—the first time this has been done—in a child of 10 in Canada…Isn't that nice? Yes, I will sleep deeply tonight."

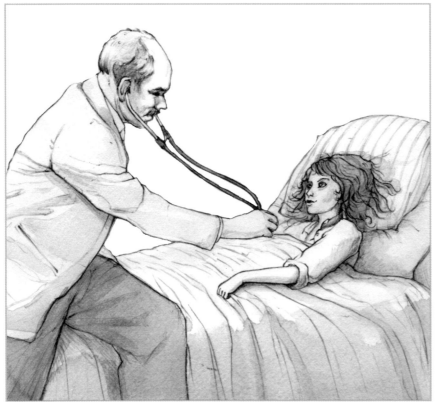

One patient of Bethune's in Montreal was a ten-year-old girl called Yvette. Her parents were poor and her case very bad. If nothing was done, Yvette would certainly die in a few weeks. Her only chance was an operation to remove her right lung. This operation had never been performed on such a young child in Canada, and the chances were strong that Yvette would die while the doctor was working.

No doctor at the hospital was prepared to risk the operation. Bethune agonized over what to do. If he did nothing, she would die. If he operated, he would probably kill her and have to tell the parents that it was his fault. But Yvette's only chance was the operation.

Bethune decided to go ahead. The operation was long and difficult, and many of the other doctors turned out to watch. Yvette almost died, but she didn't. The operation was a success.

The Famous Anger

Bethune had a sharp temper which could explode unexpectedly. Sometimes, when he was working in the operating room, he would shout

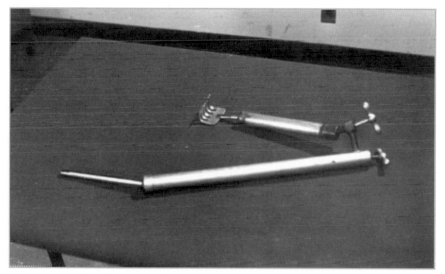

Two surgical tools invented by Norman, a scapula lifter and a retractor

loudly and hurl a surgical instrument that displeased him across the room. But his anger was often constructive. On many occasions after such an outburst, he would arrive at work a

few days later with an improved version of the instrument which had displeased him.

One instrument that particularly irritated Bethune was the rib shearers. These were used to cut through a patient's ribs to allow access to the lungs during an operation. They were inefficient and a lot of hard work to use. One day, Bethune was picking up a pair of shoes from a cobbler. The man was working on removing nails from a pair of boots, using a long-handled pair of cutters. Bethune had an idea. He bought the cutters from the surprised cobbler, had them modified and used them to cut ribs. They were so successful that they were called the Bethune Rib Shearers and are still in use in hospitals today.

But Bethune's anger was not confined to his work. Some of it was directed at Frances. In 1932, Norman and Frances divorced for a second and final time.

More Anger

Bethune painted this stern-looking portait of himself

Bethune had no patience with people whom he thought pompous or stupid. He used to take pleasure in deliberately annoying them. Once, at a dinner party given by a wealthy Montrealer, Bethune tried to cause trouble by suggesting that people should never wash, in order to allow their natural smell to come through. It was a joke, since Bethune himself was always very clean and tidy. But some people thought he was serious and were very offended.

Although he could be angry and annoying to people he thought silly, he was extremely generous to his friends. All his books had plates in them stating that this book was the property of Norman Bethune and his friends. On one occasion, someone complimented him on the woollen overcoat he was wearing. Bethune immediately removed the coat and gave it to the person as a gift.

▲▼

▼▲

The Artist

Many of Bethune's artist friends in Montreal were politically concerned and painted the unemployed asleep in the local parks or lined up at soup kitchens for free food. The artists themselves were poor and often could not afford canvas to paint on. They used to paint on brown wrapping paper scrounged from friends who worked in factories or on stretched, empty flour bags.

Bethune was a talented artist and was friends with many well-known painters in Montreal in the 1930s. He was naturally talented and assumed that he could do anything he tried. On one occasion, he was talking about this when one of his friends challenged him. To prove his point, Bethune boasted that he could have one of his paintings exhibited at the Spring Exhibition at the Art Museum in Montreal. He went away and painted *Night Operating Theatre.* Sure enough, there it was next spring amidst the work of all the famous artists.

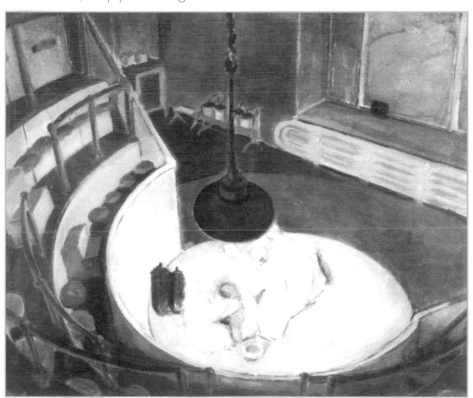

"Night Operating Theatre"

Art for Children

All through the 1930s, Canada was in the Great Depression. Crops failed all across the prairies, farms were deserted, and men were thrown out of work from Vancouver, British Columbia, to St John's, Newfoundland. With no social services, unemployed men travelled across the country on freight trains searching for work. Few found any. In the cities, the unemployed slept in filthy, overcrowded dormitories or out in the open on park benches. Montreal was no different, and these ragged men often became the models for Bethune's young artists.

Bethune may have been arrogant, but he was not selfish with his talents. On three afternoons a week and on Saturday mornings, Bethune's apartment hosted the Montreal Children's Creative Art Centre. Bethune paid all the expenses, so the lessons were free for kids, and some of the best known artists of the day helped him.

The idea was to give underprivileged children a chance to work creatively. Bethune and his artist friends would take the children to an art gallery or out onto the streets of Montreal. Then they were taken back to Bethune's apartment, given paper, brushes and paints and encouraged to paint what they had seen.

The Social Life

In the 1930s, Fascism had succeeded in Germany and Italy. It also had many supporters in Canada. These people were racist and violent. They used to march through the streets smashing the windows of shops owned by Jewish people. They also hated Communists, Socialists and anyone else who took the side of the poor and unemployed. They did not like Norman Bethune.

On one occasion, a group of Fascists broke into Bethune's apartment. They smashed his furniture and possessions, daubed swastikas (the symbol of Fascism) on his walls and destroyed the paintings done by the children in his art classes. Bethune reported the event to the police but had little hope that anything would be done to find the culprits.

Unfortunately, many of the police often took the side of the Fascists against the workers and the poor.

The apartment building where Bethune lived in Montreal

Bethune's Montreal apartment was not just used for art classes. It was also a meeting place for artists, writers and poets. When you were invited to Bethune's place for the first time, he would usher you into the bathroom. Inside were four open cans of different coloured paint. Bethune would invite you to dip your hand in the colour of your choice and make a print on the wall. Your name was then written across the palm. The wall was very soon full.

Bethune loved art, and the walls of his living room were covered with paintings. All, that is, except one wall that was kept clear. On this wall, Bethune used to write down clever or humorous sayings that came up in the course of conversation so that he could remember them later.

Caught in a riot

Bethune was not alone in feeling helpless. Many people saw the hardships of the poor, the inability of the government to do anything about it and the brutality of the police. What could one person do? Nothing, it seemed. The only answer appeared to lie in organizing and forming political parties that could change things for the better. The party with the best organization was the Communist Party, and many people who wanted to change things for the better were drawn to it.

One afternoon, while driving through Montreal, Bethune's car became stuck in a traffic jam. Thinking there might have been an accident, Bethune left his car and went to see what was going on. What he found was a demonstration by the unemployed asking for milk, bread and jobs. As Bethune watched, a line of police on horseback charged the crowd, swinging clubs wildly. There was chaos. People fled in all directions, accompanied by the sound of sirens, screams, shouts and pounding horses hooves. Many were injured and bleeding. Bethune helped those he could, but he never forgot the violence of the police that afternoon. The demonstrators were the poor and unemployed people that he treated for free and tried to help. What could he do on his own when even the police seemed to be so obviously against them?

During the Depression, unemployed men often had to line up for hours for the chance of a job so that they could provide for their families.

Communism

The Russian revolution happened in 1917 while Bethune was in the Royal Navy. The Czar was overthrown and Russia became a Communist state. Little was known in Canada about what life was like under Communism in Russia. If you didn't like Communism it was horrible, and if you did like Communism, it was wonderful. To those people who despaired of the Canadian Government ever helping the unemployed and poor, Communist Russia was a hopeful model for how society might be. After his visit there, Bethune began to see things that way too.

For most of his time in Montreal, Bethune was not a Communist. In fact, at one meeting where a speaker was telling the audience how wonderful things were in Communist Russia, Bethune had to be restrained from disrupting the meeting.

"How do you know the speaker is wrong?" a friend of Bethune's asked. "You have never been to Russia."

That calmed Bethune down, but it started him thinking. He sold his sports car and paid for a trip to a medical conference in Russia. While he was there, Bethune asked questions endlessly and tried to find out everything he could about how Communism worked. He was amazed to see that almost all the measures he had been promoting for the treatment of tuberculosis had already been put into effect. And they were working. Despite the chaos of revolution and civil war, the number of tuberculosis patients had fallen by 50% in Russia in twenty years. If they could do it, why couldn't Canada?

Medicare

In 1962, the first Medicare system in Canada was introduced in Saskatchewan. The province's doctors, descendants of the ones who had ignored Bethune and his ideas almost thirty years before, went on strike. But the people wanted Medicare. The strike collapsed, and within ten years, all Canadian provinces were part of the Medicare system. Today there are still people who want to get rid of Medicare and go back to the system of paying for a doctor's help that Bethune fought so hard against.

This newspaper headline is about a time when Bethune addressed a conference and advocated universal healthcare. No one took him seriously, but he made the news.

When Bethune returned from Russia, he joined the Canadian Communist Party, but he kept it secret, because being a Communist in those days made you an outcast. With a group of health and social workers, Bethune formed the Montreal Group for the Security of the People's Health. The group studied health care around the world and wrote a report recommending a Medicare system in Canada. Bethune did not expect the government to accept his proposals immediately, but he did expect his report to cause some trouble and get people talking. He was disappointed when it was completely ignored by politicians and doctors.

What could Bethune do? He was becoming an outcast for his outspoken views. Hardly any of his doctor colleagues would have anything to do with him. Bethune was struggling to change the world for the better, but he was misunderstood and ignored.

Surgeon Startles Medical Assembly

Feeling Depressed

In 1931, the Spanish people got rid of their king, Alfonso XIII, and established a democratic republic. They had tried to introduce education for everyone and to give land to the poverty-stricken peasants. But they had met with opposition. The landowners, the Spanish Catholic Church and the army regarded the elected government as Communist and a threat to their privilege. On July 17, 1936, the Spanish army in the colony of Morocco rose in revolt against the government and killed their opponents. They were led by General Francisco Franco but, within days, other army units all across Spain were also in revolt. There was widespread fighting in the streets of Madrid and Barcelona, and the country descended into civil war.

Some Canadian volunteers on their way to help the democratic government in Spain

In 1936, a friend met Bethune in a Montreal hotel. Norman's car was parked outside, out of gas, he looked as if he had slept in his clothes, and he carried a small bag containing a telephone book so that the hotel staff would think he had luggage. Bethune was depressed and unhappy, and he didn't know what to do. For all his adult life he had been struggling to improve conditions for those less well off than himself. He had helped lots of individuals, but the system that forced the poor and unemployed to live in unhealthy conditions was no closer to change. In fact, it was getting worse.

But there was one place in the world where the people were taking a stand against Fascism—Spain—and events there were about to pull Bethune, and many others, into the battle.

Off to Spain

The news that a Fascist revolt had broken out in Spain electrified people in Canada. Here at last was a chance to do something concrete to fight against Fascism. Many hoped that the shots being fired on Spanish streets would be the first in a war which would sweep Fascism away for good. They were wrong. The governments of Canada, Britain, the United States and France did nothing to stop Fascism's destruction of the Spanish peoples' hard-won freedom. Even when British ships were attacked by Fascist bombers and submarines, the government did nothing.

Despite their governments' disapproval, and a law in Canada that made it a criminal offense to go and fight in Spain, thousands of men and women from around the world flocked to help the Spanish Government fight the Fascist rebellion. Almost 1,600 Canadians went to Spain. Half of them never returned and lie buried in a land they thought important enough to fight for.

For a man of action like Bethune, the war in Spain was like a magnet. Here was a chance to do something. If he had any doubts, he just had to look at his fellow doctors, many of whom were openly supporting the Fascists. Bethune tried to borrow money to get to Spain. None of his friends had any. Eventually, he went to an organization that was trying to set up a medical unit to help the Spanish. If Bethune agreed to head the unit, they could give him a one-way boat ticket to Spain. It was enough. On October 24, 1936, Norman Bethune walked up the gangway of the S.S. Empress of Britain and set sail for Europe.

Posters were used to raise support for the Republic; this one condemns the German influence on Franco's Fascists.

Blood Transfusion

In 1492, the same year that Christopher Columbus sailed for the New World, the blood of three young men was given to the aged Pope Innocent VII. The experiment was a failure, and the young men and the Pope all died. It was not until the early 19th century that James Blundell carried out the first successful human-to-human blood transfusion. But it was still a very chancy business until scientists discovered that blood is of four different types, A, B, AB and O. If the wrong type of blood is used, the transfusion doesn't work.

The next discoveries were that adding sodium citrate to blood prevented it clotting and that adding sugar allowed it to be kept for up to three weeks. Bethune didn't discover any of this; it was all well-known when he went to Spain. What he did was find a new way to apply what was known and, in doing so, he saved hundreds of lives.

Republican soldiers were not as well-armed as their Fascist opponents.

Bethune arrived in Madrid, the Spanish capital, just as it was being besieged by the rebels. Fighting was going on at the edges of the city and, every night, enemy bombers flew over, destroying buildings and killing civilians.

Very rapidly, Bethune saw what was needed. He remembered all the wounded soldiers who had died in the First World War because they could not have a blood transfusion fast enough. Blood transfusion had improved since 1915, but a wounded soldier still had to live long enough to get back to an aid station to receive blood. Bethune's innovation was to take the Canadian Blood Transfusion Service right to the front lines so that the wounded could be helped as soon as possible after they were hurt. That way they would have a much better chance of surviving.

Night Work

Driving at night through the darkened streets of Madrid in December, 1936, was eerie. Bombs were falling all around, and the rifle and machine-gun fire from the fighting sounded very close.

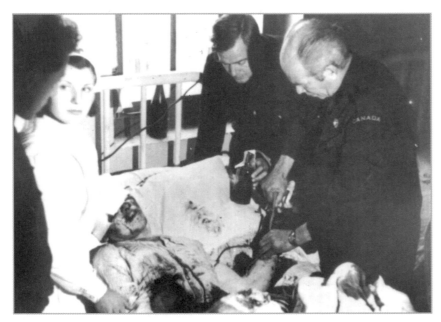

One night, Bethune took the blood transfusion unit to the front lines in a park on the edge of Madrid. Explosions were echoing nearby, and bullets were zipping through the trees above. Wounded soldiers lay everywhere. One boy appeared almost dead. He was in shock from his wound, his breathing shallow, his eyes sunken and his skin deathly pale.

Bethune crouched beside the boy and inserted a tube into his arm. The tube led to a bottle of preserved blood. The blood flowed into the wounded boy. Two bottles, a litre of blood. Then the miracle happened. The colour returned to the boy's cheeks, his teeth stopped chattering and he opened his eyes. Raising himself onto one elbow, the boy took a cigarette and said "Gracias", Spanish for thank you. He would now live long enough to have his wound attended to.

It was a simple procedure, but no one before Bethune had thought to do it so close to the fighting. It was Bethune's miracle, and he would repeat it over and over again in the streets of Madrid and in the hills around.

In Danger

The problem with taking blood close to battles was that there was always a danger of being caught up in the fighting. On one occasion, Bethune was driving to a hospital at Guadalajara, where a major battle was taking place. The car he was driving came under fire, so the occupants climbed out and crawled back to safety along a ditch. When things calmed down, Bethune returned to find a bullet hole in the car's windshield, exactly where his head would have been had he not escaped.

After the Fascist attack on Madrid failed, General Franco tried to encircle the city. There were many battles in the hills around Madrid. Guadalajara was one. These attacks also failed to capture the city, but things were not going well for the Spanish government. The Fascists in Germany and Italy were supplying arms, planes, pilots and troops to the rebels. The democracies were ignoring this and refusing to sell arms to the loyalists. Only Russia and Mexico sent aid to the Spanish government. The longer the war went on, the less chance the government had of winning.

Bethune always enjoyed being out in the wilderness. He found time while he was in Spain to do some skiing.

The Malaga Road

A man approached Bethune on the Malaga road. "My child is very ill," he said desperately. "He will die before I carry him to Almeria… I will stay behind… I ask only for him… Take him—leave him wherever there is a hospital… Tell them I will follow… Tell them this one is Juan Blas and that I will come soon to find him."

We have no way of knowing what happened to Juan Blas or his father. Did the boy survive? Were they ever reunited? If they were, it was because of Norman Bethune.

Bethune was surrounded by exhausted, ragged refugees. He was on his way to supply blood to the soldiers defending the city of Malaga. But he was too late. Malaga had fallen to the Fascists a few days before. The Fascists were now busy killing anyone who did not support them, and the refugees, many of them women and children, were trying to reach safety in the town of Almeria. Many of them were too exhausted to make it.

Bethune emptied the blood supplies out of his truck and began loading people, mostly children. His first load was forty children and two women. For four days and nights, Bethune and his assistants worked constantly helping the wounded and ferrying the exhausted to safety. Choosing whom to take and whom to leave was agonizing.

Leaving Spain

The Spanish Civil War dragged on for almost three years. Canada, Britain, France and the United States never did help the Spanish government. Germany and Italy helped the rebels to the very end. In April 1939, the Spanish Republic surrendered to General Franco's Fascist army. It was not until 1975, when Franco finally died, that Spain became a democracy again. One of its first acts was to give Spanish citizenship to all foreigners like Bethune who had come to help them in the war.

By the spring of 1937, Bethune's blood transfusion unit was working well and supplying blood to the entire front lines. Things were better organized than in the first chaotic days of the war. This didn't suit Bethune. He preferred to be free to do what he saw as important without being told what to do. He began having arguments with his superiors. It was decided that he would now be more use raising money for the Spanish cause back in Canada.

On May 18, 1937, Bethune regretfully left Madrid for Canada. He had said that the city was the centre of the world and he had been happy there, working hard amongst people who felt the same as he did and contributing to something worthwhile. It would be hard returning to Canada after that.

Bethune with the transfusion truck that saved so many lives during his time in Spain

To support the Spanish people in 1937, you did not have to go and fight. Many famous writers, actors and performers used their popularity to help the Spanish cause. Tens of thousands of people donated money to supply ambulances and equipment, anything that was needed. Countless average, decent people saw their help to the Spanish Republic as a way to do something to fight the threat of Fascism that their own governments seemed unable or unwilling to do anything about.

Back Home

At eight in the morning of June 16, 1937, the train from Toronto pulled into Montreal's Bonaventure Station. As it stopped, a crowd broke through the barriers and flooded down the platform. They surrounded the well-dressed man who had just stepped down from a carriage. They lifted him shoulder-high and carried him out of the station. In an open car, amidst cheering, banner-waving crowds and storms of bunting, the car made its triumphal way through the streets. Norman Bethune had come home.

That night Bethune spoke to a capacity crowd of 8,000 people in the Mount Royal Arena. He told them about Spain, about his experiences, about the Spanish people's struggle to stay free from Fascism, and he told the crowd about the need for money to support that struggle. He raised $2,000 the one evening.

A Spellbinding Speaker

During his speaking tour, Bethune finally announced publicly that he was a member of the Communist Party of Canada. Now he was completely separated from his doctor colleagues. He could never have a successful career in Canada. When he visited the Catholic Sacré-Cœur Hospital, where he had been head of the chest surgery unit before he went to Spain, the Mother Superior refused to meet him, thinking that he was the devil. The war in Spain was going badly, and Bethune couldn't go back there. Since he had announced he was a Communist, he couldn't work in Canada. Where could he go and what could he do? For a third time, events on the other side of the world were going to give Norman Bethune an opportunity.

Over the six months following his return from Spain, Bethune criss-crossed the country speaking, sometimes twice a day, to anyone who would listen. Sometimes he spoke to a handful of listeners in a town hall; sometimes he spoke to thousands in a hockey arena. Each time his message was the same. He told them about the Malaga Road; he spoke against his own government, which appeared to be doing nothing; and he warned that Fascism in Canada was just around the corner. He was always captivating.

One night, a fourteen-year-old boy went to see Bethune because he was curious and had nothing else to do. He took a dime, the only money he had in the world, to buy a milkshake. He didn't buy a milkshake. He gave his dime to Norman Bethune to help Spanish boys his own age who were fighting against Fascism. As an old man, that boy still vividly remembered the night he heard Norman Bethune speak, and he retained his admiration for him all his life.

Bethune's strong new views and his Spanish experiences gave him the courage to speak out about the threat of Fascism.

A Dedicated Man

On July 7, 1937, while Bethune was speaking in Timmins, Ontario, the Japanese army invaded China. Japan at the time had an Emperor but was controlled by its army, and the army wanted an Empire. In 1931 they had taken Manchuria away from China, now they wanted the rest. At first the Japanese swept through China and captured the capital Nanjing, where they murdered 350,000 people. The Chinese army was no match for the ruthless, efficient Japanese soldiers. The exception was the Communist Eighth Route Army led by Mao Zedong. They were not well equipped, but they were battle hardened after years of fighting against the Chinese government. Now they controlled a large, remote area in Northern China where they fought desperately to stop the Japanese invaders. That was where Bethune could help best.

Late in 1937, Norman Bethune finally found his cause. He was forty-seven. He had no children. After the departure of Frances, his personal life was empty. His career was in ruins. All the things that had been important in his life before—his partying, his art collection, his medical practice—seemed irrelevant. All that was left was the fight against Fascism. Fascism was a disease, just as deadly as the tuberculosis he had fought so long to eradicate. And it had to be fought just as ruthlessly. Bethune was a brilliant, innovative doctor and Spain had toughened him. Where could he do most good? The answer lay across the Pacific Ocean.

This famous photo shows Bethune on the Great Wall of China.

What Bethune saw in China made him angry and bitter. He blamed the government of Canada for not helping the Chinese in their struggle against the Japanese invaders. He felt that he was not a Canadian any more, but a citizen of the world taking part in a revolution to change things for the better. He wrote: "I refuse to live in a world that spawns murder and corruption without raising my hand against them. I refuse to condone, by passivity, or by default, the wars which greedy men make against others."

A Close Call

In March, 1938, newspapers in Canada announced that Norman Bethune was dead. They were almost right.

While travelling north to meet up with the Communist army, Bethune had been caught up in a major Japanese attack. For days Bethune had walked, only hours ahead of the advancing enemy. He was surrounded by a chaos of refugees and retreating Chinese soldiers, but still he managed to treat the sick and wounded. At every village, lines of the sick appeared as word spread that a doctor was there. Once, Bethune was in a hillside cave treating a child with convulsions. All at once, the mother rushed out into the open, screaming the child's name at the top of her voice. A surprised Bethune was told by the locals that the woman believed the child's soul had left its body, and she was calling it back. Whatever the reason, the child recovered.

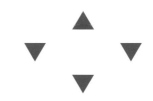

Bethune examines a Chinese boy, one of the innocent victims of war.

Building Hospitals

When Bethune at last reached the area controlled by the Communist army, he met their leader, Mao Zedong. They got along well and talked all through the night. Then Bethune moved farther north, to Sung-yen K'ou, where he built a hospital. Unfortunately, three weeks after the hospital opened, it was attacked by the Japanese and destroyed.

This Chinese painting shows the meeting between Bethune and Mao.

Bethune moved even farther north. There he built another hospital. But this time it was one that the Japanese couldn't destroy. Bethune's new hospital had an operating table and all the equipment Bethune had brought with him, but it was mobile. Everything could be folded down and packed onto three mules which could be led over the roughest mountain paths. The operating room could be set up in any peasant's hut or a Buddhist Temple—wherever the fighting was fiercest. Bethune's watchword became, "Go to the wounded. Don't wait for the wounded to come to you."

Mao Zedong (or Tse-tung, as Bethune spelled it) was born in Hunan Province on Boxing Day, 1893. In 1935, he became head of the outlawed Chinese Communist Party and led his soldiers on an epic Long March across China to escape the Government forces. After the Japanese were defeated in World War Two, Mao kept fighting and became the head of a Chinese Communist government in 1949. He ruled China until his death in September 1976.

52

Bethune's Miracle Again

A painting of Bethune demonstrating his transfusion "miracle" in China

A problem Bethune had in China was convincing the local populace to donate blood for his operations. The peasants didn't understand and were afraid. In one village, Bethune saw an opportunity. A soldier had been brought in from nearby fighting. He was only lightly wounded but had lost a lot of blood. The man lay grey, cold and apparently dead on a stretcher in the village square. With a good sense of drama, Bethune called the entire village out to watch. As he explained what he was doing, Bethune rolled up his sleeve and donated some of his blood directly into the wounded man. As the villagers watched in awe, the "dead" man quivered, groaned, opened his eyes and smiled. It was the Spanish miracle all over again. Bethune never had trouble finding donors again.

A Hard Life

Bethune had a young personal aid, Ho Tzu-hsin, to look after him. The boy found it very difficult to boil an egg the way Bethune liked it. With his characteristic determination, Bethune undertook the long task of teaching Ho Tzu-hsin how to cook an egg just right. When the boy succeeded, Bethune had their picture taken together with the egg.

Life in the remote mountains with the Chinese peasants and soldiers was incredibly hard. The heat in summer was unbearable and the winter was bitter cold. The villages had no electricity or running water, and the food was unfamiliar and the same every day. The life was so hard that, after a year in China, Bethune looked as if he had aged ten years.

He missed books and conversation in his own language. He dreamed of coffee, roast beef and apple pie and ice cream. He wrote to a friend, "I wish we had a radio and a hamburger sandwich."

But just as he had been amongst the bombs in Spain, Bethune was happy. He was doing something worthwhile, and that made all the hardship worth it. He wrote: "I don't think I have been so happy for a long time. I am content. I am doing what I want to do."

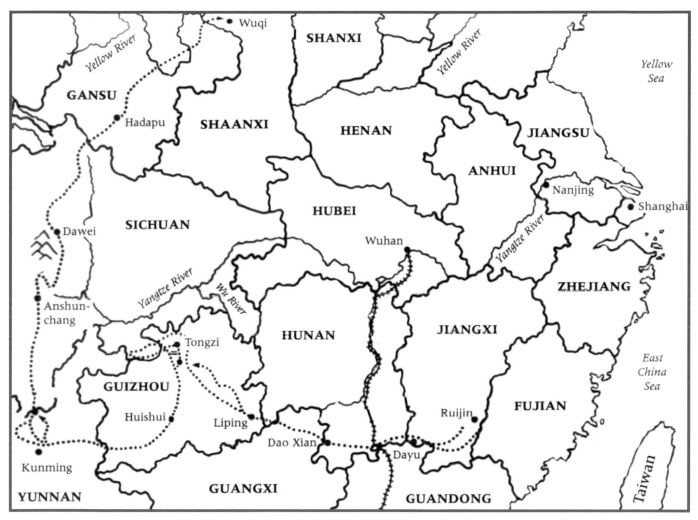

The Communists' Long March, 1934-35

The dotted line shows the vast distance marched almost non-stop by Mao's Red Army when they were pursued by the government armies. The place where Bethune worked in 1938 was near the Communists' base at the end of the March (top left).

(note: The spellings on the map of modern China are the modern spellings of Chinese in English and are different to those used in Norman's time. The exception is the Yangtze River, which is still the most commonly recognized name)

The Famous Anger

Bethune didn't leave his anger behind when he sailed for China. He was unforgiving whenever he came upon incompetence. In one village, he discovered a hospital full of wounded people in the most awful condition. Bandages hadn't been changed, and there was dirt everywhere. "Who is responsible for this?" Bethune roared. A sheepish Dr. Fong came forward, and Bethune berated the poor man mercilessly. How could Fong call himself a doctor? He was incompetent, a disgrace to the medical profession and a danger to the brave soldiers who were risking their lives to fight the invaders. Fong stood silent. Then Bethune set about doing what he could for the wounded.

Later, Bethune learned Fong's story. Fong wasn't really a doctor at all—he was a poor peasant whose job had been to tend to the water buffalo for his village. He had joined the

continued on next page ⟶

Sometimes Bethune's anger was directed back across the Pacific. In May, 1938, he wrote: "Canada must help these people They have fought for the salvation of China and the liberation of Asia." After complaining that he had heard nothing for five months, despite "repeated telegrams and letters", Bethune went on: "I can give no explanation to Mao Tse-tung—I am ashamed."

Communist army as a guard and, through reading late at night and watching the nurses and doctors around him, he had taught himself the basics of medical care. He had become a nurse and then, because there had been no one else, he had become a surgeon. Before Bethune arrived at his hospital, Fong had been learning a few words of English so that he could learn a little more from the famous foreign doctor who was coming to his village.

Bethune felt bad that he had been so harsh. When he returned, Bethune sought out Fong and asked him to join his unit. If he wanted to learn that badly, then Bethune would teach him. And Fong did learn. A year later, when Bethune was dying, Dr. Fong was one of the few people to whom Bethune left some of his precious surgical instruments.

Bethune made many friends in China amongst his comrades.

Working Close to the Enemy

Frequently, Bethune and his team operated within sound of the Japanese guns. Occasionally, the fighting was much closer.

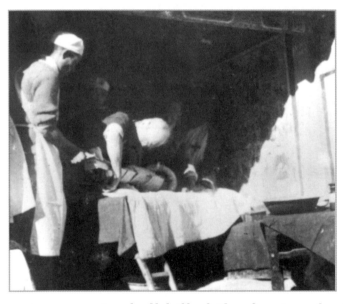

Bethune operating in China

Once, Bethune was working in a Buddhist Temple as Japanese shells exploded all around. He performed 115 operations in 69 hours, the last fifteen with the patients strapped down to the table because they had run out of anesthetic. Everyone tried to persuade him to leave, but Bethune refused as long as there was a single wounded man needing his attention.

At one point in the marathon, Bethune noticed the man in charge of the hospital hovering at his shoulder. "Why are you here?" he asked. The man explained that, if a shell killed the foreign doctor, he would be blamed for not taking him to safety. Since it was hopeless to argue with Bethune, the man had decided to stay as close as possible to him so that, if a shell did hit the temple, no one could accuse him of being safe while his charge was in danger.

When the last soldier had been cared for, an exhausted Bethune staggered out of the temple to find the surrounding village nothing more than a heap of smoking ruins.

The End

Bethune was conscious right to the end. On November 11, he wrote to Lang Lin, his interpreter: "I came back from the front yesterday. There was no good in being there. I couldn't get out of bed or operate...useless for work. Vomiting on stretcher all day. High fever, over 40C... Can't get to sleep, mentally very bright... I feel freely today. Pain over heart... Will see you tomorrow, I expect." But there was no tomorrow. This was Bethune's last letter. Within hours he was dead.

On October 28, 1939, Bethune was operating on a soldier with a broken leg. As he was working, his chisel slipped and sliced open the middle finger of his left hand. It was not an unusual occurrence, given the primitive working conditions, so Bethune had his hand bandaged and continued work. But something different happened this time. Several days later, Bethune was operating on a soldier with a long-untreated head wound. He was working without gloves, since they had none, and the head wound was infected. Some of the infection got into the cut on Bethune's finger.

By November 5, Bethune's finger was infected and he was running a fever. He had blood poisoning, and without antibiotics, there was nothing anyone could do. He became steadily worse and, at 5:20 on the morning of November 12, 1939, Norman Bethune died.

This impressive stone statue of Bethune in China was put up after his death. Bethune had become a hero to a whole nation.

Remembered in China

When he heard of Bethune's death,
Mao Zedong wrote:
"I am deeply grieved over his death.
Now we are all commemorating him,
which shows how profoundly his spirit
inspires everyone."

Bethune's body was carried over the mountains and laid to rest in Chu-ch'eng, where ten thousand people, many weeping, filed past to say good-bye. The peasants built an elaborate tomb, but Bethune's body had to be moved when the tomb was destroyed by the Japanese.

Today, Bethune's body is buried in a memorial park across the road from the large Norman Bethune International Peace Hospital. Hundreds of thousands of people visit the park each year. Bethune's memory is revered by millions of Chinese people.

These Chinese stamps commemorate Bethune's contribution to their cause.

Remembered in Canada

This Canadian stamp celebrating Bethune's life was produced in 1990

Because he was a Communist, and people were frightened of Communists, it took longer for Norman Bethune to be recognized in Canada. It was not until the 1970s that books and movies about his life became readily available. The house where he was born in Gravenhurst was restored and turned into a museum. Now he is considered to be of "national historic significance." If he were alive today, he would laugh at that, since it makes him sound like a ruined castle. Then he would point out that the things he fought for were not just dry footnotes in history books, but real causes which affected the lives and deaths of thousands of real people. Then he would leave, pointing out that there are just as many battles against injustice to be fought today as there were when the enemies were tuberculosis and Fascism.

The old Bethune home in Gravenhurst was opened as an historic site in 1976.

Bethune
Comes Home

In August of the year 2000, a two-metre high bronze statue of Norman Bethune was unveiled in front of the opera house in downtown Gravenhurst. Funded by government grants, local business and private sponsors, and donations from medical schools in China, it was unveiled by Adrienne Clarkson, Canada's first Governor-General of Chinese ancestry. Norman Bethune has come home.

Bethune's life and times

1890   Norman Bethune is born in Gravenhurst, Ontario.

1901   Bethune's future wife, Frances Campbell Penney, is born.

1907   Bethune graduates from school and goes to work as a lumberjack.

1909   Bethune works as a public school teacher and attends the University of Toronto.

1911   Bethune works as a teacher of adults for the Reading Camp Association in logging camps.

1914   The First World War begins and Norman Bethune enlists in the medical corps.

1915   Bethune is a stretcher bearer and participates in battles at Ypres. He is injured and sent away from the front.

1916   Bethune receives his Bachelor of Medicine and starts his own practice.

1917	Bethune receives a white feather and is shamed into reenlisting, this time in the Navy. The Russian Revolution overthrows the Czar.
1918	The First World War finally ends.
1919	Bethune interns at Great Ormond Street Hospital in London, England, then returns home to Ontario.
1922	Mussolini's Fascists seize power in Italy and the U.S.S.R. is formed out of Russia and surrounding countries.
1923/24	Norman and Frances are married. Bethune opens a practice in Detroit, Michigan.
1926	Bethune contracts tuberculosis. Frances leaves him. His recovery from the disease takes over a year.
1927	Bethune has his lung collapsed and is healed. After more training, he moves to Montreal.
1929	Bethune and Frances remarry. The Great Depression begins with the collapse of the New York Stock Exchange.
1931	The King of Spain is overthrown and a Republican government is formed. The Japanese invade Manchuria.

1932	Frances divorces Bethune again. The Nazis form the government in Germany.
1935	Bethune visits the U.S.S.R. and on his return joins the Communist Party of Canada.
1936	Bethune advocates national health care in Canada, then leaves for Spain to help in the fiercely raging Civil War.
1937	Bethune travels Canada lecturing to raise money for the Republicans in Spain. Japan invades China.
1938	Bethune travels to China and journies to the Communist headquarters. He builds his model hospital, which is destroyed by the Japanese.
1939	The Spanish Republic surrenders to Franco's Fascists. The Second World War begins. Bethune cuts his finger and contracts blood poisoning. Norman Bethune dies.
1949	Mao Zedong's forces defeat the Nationalists and form the Chinese government.
1952	Bethune's remains are moved to a new park.
1976	The Bethune house in Gravenhurst is opened as a national memorial.

About the author

John Wilson, who was born in Scotland, is the author of numerous successful books for children, including the *Weet* trilogy (Napoleon Publishing), *Across Frozen Seas* (Beach Holme Publishing), *Ghosts of James Bay* (Beach Holme) and *Lost in Spain* (Fitzhenry and Whiteside), a novel about the Spanish Civil War. He is also the author of two young adult biographies, including another book about Bethune, *A Life of Passionate Conviction*, and a biography of Sir John Franklin, *Traveller Over Undiscovered Seas* (XYZ Publishing).

John Wilson currently lives with his wife and children on Vancouver Island. *Righting Wrongs* is his first children's biography for Napoleon. His next endeavour is a young adult novel set during the First World War.

The author used the following books in researching this story:

The Mind of Norman Bethune by Roderick Stewart (Toronto: Fitzhenry and Whiteside, 1977)

The Scalpel, The Sword by Ted Allan and Sydney Gordon (Toronto: McClelland and Stewart, 1952)

Bethune by Roderick Stewart (Toronto: New Press, 1973)

Norman Bethune: his Times and his Legacy by David A.E. Shepard and Andrée Levesque (editors)

Bethune: The Montreal Years by Wendell McLeon, Libbie Park and Stanley Ryerson (Toronto: James Lorimer, 1978)

The Gallant Cause: Canadians In The Spanish Civil War by Mark Zuelke (Vancouver: Whitecap Books, 1996)

A Concise History of the Spanish Civil War by Gabriel Jackson (London: Thames and Hudson, 1974)

Photo and Art Credits

Bethune and his times on the Internet

There is quite a lot of history to be found on the Internet. More information on Bethune and the times he lived in can be found on these sites.

Bethune

Friends of Bethune
Information on the Bethune House Museum in Gravenhurst
www.friendsofbethune.on.ca

An Internet biography of Bethune
www.sd83.bc.ca/stu/9806/mabf1.html

Tuberculosis

Information about TB in Canada. Surprisingly, it doesn't mention Bethune, but it is a good overview of the history of the fight against TB.
www.lung.ca/tb

Spain and the Spanish Civil War

www.sispain.org   *A good introduction to the history and culture of Spain*
www.geocities.com/CapitolHill/9820   *A detailed history of the Spanish Civil War*
www.cyberspain.com   *Another general interest site about Spain*

China and its Civil War

www.cnd.org/fairbank/prc.html   *A history of the People's Republic of China under Mao*
www.china-contact.com/www/history.html   *If you are interested in China, this site gives a very quick overview of Chinese history up to Mao's time*
www.iisg.nl/~landsberger   *An interesting site of propaganda art from the People's Republic, which shows how Mao spread his theories*

Note: The internet changes every day. At the time that this book was printed, all of these sites were available. However, we can't guarantee that they will always be there. If any aren't, a simple keyword search will probably take you to information on Bethune and his times.

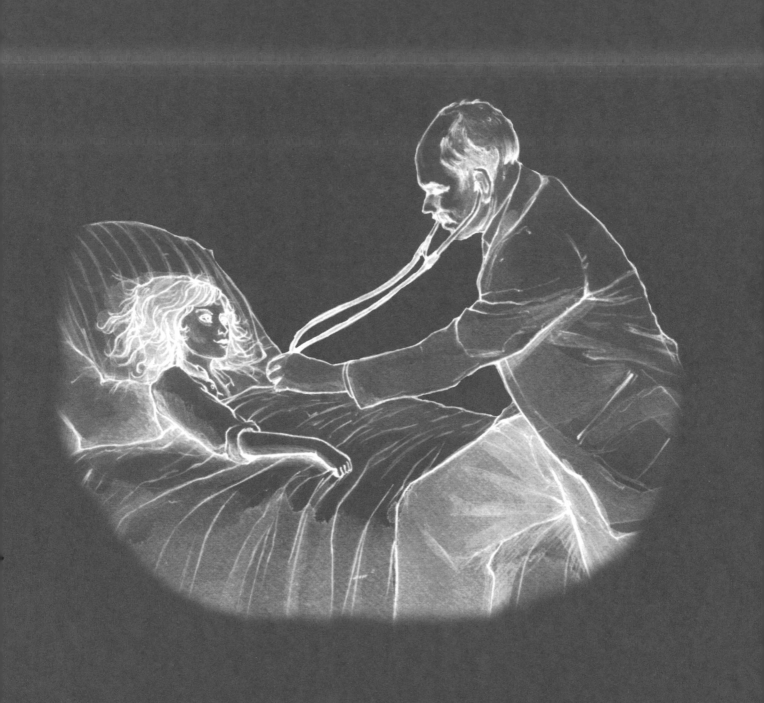